WAITING
FOR A
SIGN

∽— A Ramble Through Life —∽

Cole Smith

ISBN-13: 978-1500571283
ISBN-10: 1500571288

CONTENTS

INTRODUCTION

My male ancestors lived to be old men. I remember my
paternal granddad. He was a rangy old guy with a full
head of silver hair "fine as silk," or so my bald-headed father
would comment. Grandpa still wore it in a pompadour till the
day he died and still worked as a logger with his younger son
deep into old age. I only had one conversation with him that
I remember. I was eight or ten years old and in his open-sided
woodshed trying to sharpen my little hunting knife. He came
in to put an edge on his double-bitted axe before going into the
woods and took over the sharpening job on my knife. After he
handed it back, I was testing the edge while he worked on his
axe. He was in his 70's, and I asked him when he was going to
quit working. "Oh hell," he said, "If I quit I'll just die." And, that
is about the way it worked out.

I've never given much thought to all the family tree
stuff that is going around now, but off and on during my life
I have wondered what kind of a life Grandpa led. I know he
married above his station, according to Grandmother, and I
know she never let him forget it. He did get even with her on

his deathbed when he said, "Mabel, why don't you get out of here and let me die in peace." I wish he had written down some stuff about his days on this earth. I think they would have made interesting reading. I remember everyone was a little shocked to find a set of brass knuckles when they were doing the post-death divvy-up. His uncles fought in the Civil War and spent time in Andersonville prison, and he came west, out of Indiana and Kansas, as a little kid on a wagon train. At least partway until they got to the railhead.

Anyway, I now have a grandson, and I now am an old man. My life has not been nearly as interesting as I am sure my granddad's was, but I will be as distant from my grandson as my grandpa was from me, and because of that I have written down a few stories for him.

So, kid, if you are reading this, and if you waited as long as I did to get interested in the guys that came before you, I am sure I am a long time gone. And, just so you know, I never did get comfortable with my life. I was always waiting for a sign, waiting for a deep voice to come down out of the ether and say something like "Cole, here is what I want you to do with your life." It never came, so I just kind of muddled through. Now, I have this recurring daytime nightmare where I see myself dozing in my chair in an assisted living facility, drooling on my bib, and the voice finally comes, *"Cole, sorry to be so late getting to you, been busy. Anyway, here is what I want you to do with your life."* I just know I am going to have that deer-in-the-headlights look.

THE FISH

People tell me they have memories from when they were two or three years old. I think I may have those memories, but they are just snippets and fragments. My first real memory was with this fish that hung out in the small turbulent waters at the outlet of a culvert. The culvert ran under the county road on my parent's farm in western Washington. I must have been at least five years old, because I was free on the earth.

I don't remember how I became aware of that fish, but I do remember the electric shock that ran up my arm when he slammed the worm I lowered into that little maelstrom. The worm was carefully threaded onto a bent pin tied to a short length of string, and the string was wrapped around one of my smallish fingers. Because there was no barb on the bent pin, playing the fish was a short-lived affair, with me squatted on the very edge of the churning pool below the culvert, and the fish frantically stealing my bait. I think this went on for a period of time because there was more than a casual relationship between me and that fish.

Part of this memory is my very first look at a real fishhook.

My dad and I were in my grandparents' house. They were very ancient, and to me, distant people. Their house smelled different, and quiet, strange music played on the radio. I didn't get too far from my dad's leg, but somehow during the visit I got my hands on a fishhook and a short piece of fishing line. While doing the three mile drive home (I think we were in a Model A pickup), I studied the hook and knew the jig was up for that fish.

I wish this memory were clearer because I would like to understand why I had a half-gallon glass jug with me when I yarded that thrashing fish out and deposited him in the water-filled container and screwed the lid on. There was elation, I can tell you, when I trotted downstream to the little bridge carrying the jug with a frantic fish inside, and then around and up into the yard. One of my older brothers was in the driveway washing his 1935, three-windowed Ford coupe (he was dating what I considered a cow-eyed woman), and he intercepted my triumphant march to the house. After studying the fish through the glass, he crushed my world by telling me it was too small, and I needed to release it.

This fish story could be, and actually pretty much is, a blueprint of my life. Just when I think I've got a pretty good grip on the golden ring, it slips away.

I'm old now. Probably older than my grandparents were when I was studying them from behind my father's leg. I wasn't aware of it at that point, but I was within 10 feet of the big wood cooking stove with an oven lid upon which the doctor had deposited my newborn body, pronouncing me dead on arrival – DOA. He then went into the next room to administer to my mom who was having post-birth problems. After he left, I let out a screech, evidently deciding to go ahead and do another tour on earth.

Now, my own death is no longer an abstract thought like it has always been. I can see it out there, and know it is coming. I mentioned this to a young friend recently, and he told me there is a song called "Slow Train Coming." I need to listen to it.

But as Gus says at the end of his life in *Lonesome Dove*, "It was a hell of a party." And, unlike Gus, I am not nearly that dead yet.

WAITING FOR A SIGN

THE AVIATOR

B rady, my next older brother, was born with the desire to get airborne. In 1947, at the age of seven, he was serious. I remember squatting in the gravel watching while he fabricated his first pair of wings out of a sheet of plywood that he had scrounged from the tiny garage next to the county road on the dairy farm. I wasn't involved in the whole build-out because there were some salmonberries growing just around the corner of that garage, but I would check in on him from time to time.

Salmonberries were a passion of mine at the time. They were a nice orangey-yellow color when ripe and were much mellower than the prolific blackberries that would nearly cover an abandoned building in one year. Also, salmonberries were less acidic and more abundant than the huckleberries, and better all around than the black caps. That place was overrun with berries. I only needed to beat the birds and bugs to them.

I don't know if this is a thought I have acquired with 60-plus years of experience, or if I was prescient, but watching him building a wing for each arm, rather than one spanning both, seemed not quite right to me. He may have paid more attention to the birds than I had, but at any rate, he ended up with a nicely shaped elliptical wing attached to each arm, something along the lines of the English Spitfire of World War II fame.

His launch date coincided with my biting into an overripe salmonberry with a "thousand-legged" critter inside, so I had abandoned the berries and was acting as a pit boss when he climbed up on top that little garage. Ol' Brady never lacked for guts. About 25 years later he would come home from Vietnam with a briefcase bulging with air medals and dirty socks. On this day, he ran the length of the ridge and launched, and his engineering failure probably saved his life. I was standing underneath, but just off to the side, when he accelerated off the ridge. If he had built a spar connecting the two wings, plus any kind of a horizontal stabilizer, his trajectory would probably have taken him out onto the county road where he most likely would have broken his neck.

As it was, there was a momentary pause in his forward momentum, and then, with not much resistance, his legs and feet started a swing down at about the time the nicely built wings folded up with a clap, right behind his back, taking his arms with them. He hit the ground just next to me, first his heels and then his back. So there he was, gasping, a lot like a fish that has been removed from his natural element, but already planning a redesign, and it included me.

I suppose in any endeavor of this kind there comes a time

when an entrepreneur realizes he cannot do it all, so Brady must have realized he could be the designer and engineer, but would need to bring in a test pilot. And there I was, all five years of me, with salmonberry juice on my chin.

The next launch took place in the big barn. There was more than one level in that place, and the lessons learned from that first flight had evidently permeated Brady's brain because he had built a spar and a horizontal stabilizer, of sorts. When he strapped me in I imagine I looked a lot like Old Jesus did up on top of Golgotha, arms out 90 degrees on each side and attached to a bunch of lumber, with eternity staring me in the face.

The actual flight did not last all that long, and I am pretty sure the launch included an assist from Brady. I did learn one important lesson about flaring prior to landing. When that floor of baled hay surged up towards me I instinctively jerked my head back and it must have changed the angle of attack on those plywood wings, so instead of ripping my face off, it just sandpapered my chest and stomach.

WAITING FOR A SIGN

MONSTERS AND THE NIGHT WATCH

That big house on the dairy farm was a good place during the daylight hours, but when the sun went down, you did not want to live there. It was bad enough that the evening fog would creep up from the river towards the barn and house, and that the cars would quit going by on the county road, but what made it really bad was that Brady and I had a room upstairs, by the attic.

Brady slept like an old dog, so it fell to me to keep the monsters at bay, and they lived in the attic, under the eaves. The door to that place was in our room, did not have a latch, and moved slightly when they breathed. Each night, my other older brothers, who had a room back down at the head of the stairs, would listen to two radio dramas, "The Squeaking Door" and "The Shadow." I could hear every raspy voice, squeak, and heavy breath from their radio drifting over the top of the stairway, making their way into our room through the partly closed door and through an army blanket, my pillow and the hand I had clapped over my ear.

When the show ended and I was sufficiently terrified, they would shut the radio off, and the house would go dark and silent. My hand would come off my ear and I would slide very slowly up so I could look in the direction of the attic door, and the vigil would commence. I knew I only had to doze a little and the monsters would slip out on feathery feet and be on Brady and I. As the night wore on, I could hear them in there shuffling around on the creaking joists, and I could hear their breathing.

I don't remember anyone commenting on the dark circles under my eyes or my frayed nerves, but at some point my dad starved out on that dairy, and we moved back down the river to the little house on the stump ranch, next to Grandpa's place. It was small and we were poor, but it was a happy place. And the best thing was that there was not even room for us kids, let alone any monsters in the attic.

I was pretty much back to normal, running through the woods by day and sleeping all night, with only the occasional thought that the monsters might have followed us there and moved under my bed. That is when my parents had to leave for two days, and they left me with Buzz. I don't know where my sisters were, and Brady was never around when you needed him.

Buzz, another brother, was 16 years old. He had the build of a smallish weight lifter, without ever having lifted weights, still had all his hair, and owned a '41 Buick convertible. In my heart,

I knew this was not a good idea, and my worries were confirmed when he dropped me off in town, six miles from home, at the Avalon Theater. It was dark and raining. I was a country boy, not a town kid, and I don't think I had ever been in that theater. He said he would be there to pick me up when the movie finished. It was a Sunday night, so I was the only kid in the place, and there were not many grownups either. After the newsreels came the previews, then "Tom and Jerry." I was actually starting to relax a bit when the B-Western came on, and I got a little critical of the posse's riding ability, with their flapping elbows (we had horses).

What happened next did not look good, and I started getting a sinking feeling. The main feature began, and this guy pulled his boat into a lagoon that was surrounded by swamp grass and dreary looking trees. Everything was kind of dark, which is a pretty good indication that things are not as they should be. Then, a woman in a white bathing suit came out of the boat's cabin and dove overboard. When you have been on monster-watch as long as I had been, you get a feel for these things, and that is when I started sliding down behind the seat. My eyes were still just above the seat back in front of me, in that mostly deserted theater, when something stirred way down in the murky depths, and I went all the way to the floor.

I wanted to stay down there, but found my nose sliding up between the seats in front, until my eyeballs rose just above the seatback, and the hair actually stood up on top my head. This monster – that was very similar to the ones that had lived in the attic – was swimming just under the lady in the white bathing suit, and was reaching for her foot. I damn near passed out.

After about two lifetimes, they turned the lights on and I shuffled outside, into the dark and the rain. All those grownups walked away, and there I stood, a little kid in front of a darkened theater. At that time, there was not even a stoplight in that town, and the streetlights were dim. After a couple more lifetimes had passed, every nerve ending in my body was thumping, and I was about ready to bolt through the inky rain down one of those deserted streets in the direction I thought home might be when Buzz rolled around the corner and stopped in front of the theater.

Riding home, listening to the growl of the straight eight under the hood of that Buick and casting an occasional glance over at Buzz, illuminated by the soft glow of the dash lights, my nerves started calming, and my body started absorbing the many doses of adrenaline my mind had injected. Even though I was getting comfortable, I decided it would be a good idea to check for big wet footprints on the stairs to the bedroom. Just in case.

THE CHRISTIAN

Our farm was a long way from town back in the late 40s. My dad was hanging on by his teeth on that leased dairy farm, fighting brucellosis, and my mom must have been completely in over her head trying to keep body and soul together providing for nine kids, laboring over a wood cooking stove and a subpar washing machine.

Somewhere in there, this outfit came by promising salvation. All my mom and dad had to do was to load us kids on a bus on Sunday morning and send us off to town for a bout of Sunday school teachings and a serious sermon.

It wasn't much of a choice. We could work on the farm half a day Sunday, or get on the bus and get a dose of Christian teachings. I wasn't 7 years yet, but I was not an idiot. A bus ride and some hang time in Sunday school worked for me, especially when Brady, my older brother by two years, opted for it as well. Brady was not only my mentor but also a taciturn, smart and tough guy. I think he was eight years old then.

I'll tell you this much, I was not prepared for that place in town. Those people were Holy Rollers. Sunday school was only slightly intimidating. A Miss Jordic eased us country kids into an indoctrination of the finer points of the canonized version of Jesus and his followers. Once through that, with Sunday school over, we were ushered out into the main body of that place, and the sermon began, and I damn near died of fright.

This big cadaverous guy, wearing a black robe that made him look like a crow, and screaming, got up behind the pulpit and put the fear of God into me, and I do mean the fear.

Riding home on the bus, muttering Jesus over and over, I was not confirming his finer points.

Next Sunday we were back, Brady having decided we were up to the mental challenge. In addition to the town sheep, there were these other guys in there, the Rodson brothers. They were gangly, with roundish heads and close-cropped hair. They looked tough.

Partway through Miss Jordic's version of the happenings around the Sea of Galilee, Brady and the Rodson brothers dropped down behind the benches and slithered out of Sunday school. I was caught off-guard and was too scared to follow. Then, they took the dimes that were supposed to be for the collection plate and went up to Heald's Soda Shop and bought Cracker Jacks. And I was left there alone with the group of sheep that subscribed to this version of creation, and then I had to go out into the general congregation and let the crow scare me nearly to death, again.

If you have ever gotten to that place in life where you

finally say okay, this is where I take the shot, I was there the next Sunday. The idea of totally defying authority was completely foreign to me, but I was not going to spend another post-Sunday school period being traumatized by that maniac behind the pulpit. And it did not matter that I was totally paralyzed at the prospect of defying authority. When Miss Jordic turned to the blackboard to elaborate on one of her finer points, and Brady and the Rodson boys dropped behind the benches, I was nose to shoe leather all the way out the door.

Talk about liberation! I don't know if you have ever swaggered into a soda shop with 10 cents of cash money in your pants and bought a box of Cracker Jacks, all the while hanging with a tough and chancy crew, but there I was. It was a heady deal. Just before the bus left, after the sermon, we slid back into the crowd and boarded. Immediately, I was convinced we were a bunch of edgy, modern-day swashbucklers. This went on for a while. Not only were we sidestepping the hard labor of a Sunday morning on the farm, we were living the high life at Heald's.

I imagine even Blackbeard must have known that the good times could not last forever. That thought was poking me in the back of the head on that Sunday morning when Miss Jordic fingered me for the role of a shepherd in the upcoming Sunday school pageant.

I had been born with a bad case of stage fright. The thought of wrapping up in a sheet and carrying a shepherd's hook around on that stage, in front of those gray, severe and jumpy people that took in the Sunday sermons, turned my guts to water. This was a traumatic time. My dad was not the guy to approach about this madness. He was distant, and he had his hands full with sick cows and all the other unsavory things that come with being a grownup.

My mom, who was a tired and totally overworked woman, seemed more susceptible. For some reason, I had believed she wanted me at that church, so after agonizing over my decision for a week, I bucked up my courage on a Saturday morning, and told her that no way would I be in that play, and, besides that, I wasn't going back to that church ever again.

And she said, "Oh, okay. That's okay."

I was thunder struck, but on further contemplation, realized I had known all along she was a wise and benevolent person.

THE STORE-BOUGHT ARROW

Town kids made me nervous. They always seemed a little more destructive than necessary. I've read that in England during the Dark Ages, every male, starting at the age of seven, had to pull and loose a certain number of arrows each day. The French finally grasped the significance of this policy in the mud of Agincourt. An English archer didn't aim. He pulled to his ear and understood the trajectory of the arrow before he let it go.

There was a real shortage of store-bought stuff around our place in the early 50s, so if you wanted something, you had better be able to build it. I was interested in killing ruffled grouse, and I didn't have a .22 rifle yet, so I got into the bow-and-arrow business. There was an abundance of vine maple and dead and dried straight-grained, old-growth red cedar. The vine maple made a springy bow, and the cedar could be whittled down for an arrow with a fencing staple tapped over the business end, and a nock cut for the string. With no fletching, this arrow fishtailed a little in flight, but I had given so many ruffled grouse a near look at eternity that, like an English archer, I too knew where the arrow was going when I loosed.

That this homemade bow and arrow had killing power, I can attest to. Once, after a heated argument with my brother Brady (who would bequeath the '41 Ford to me a few years later), we squared off in the empty haymow in front of the workhorse stables. Somehow, he had gotten ahold of my latest series of bow and arrows, so I was verbally abusing him from behind an old overturned table. At some point, I decided to peek over the top of the table to see what affect my salty words were having on him. My move coincided with the cedar arrow already en-route, and my forehead met the arrow about 3 inches above the lip of that table. I am not sure how long I was asleep, but when I woke up with a big goose egg square in the middle of my forehead, my bow and arrow were right next to my right hand and my brother was long gone.

I don't remember how I ended up with that store-bought arrow. It had a target point, was perfectly round, had two green painted broad stripes, and had fletching. I knew it was a killer, so was holding it in reserve when those kids came up from town.

Bringing the milk cows down out of the woods was my evening chore. The route usually brought us through the verdant flat this side of Switchback Canyon, full of foxgloves, alder, glossy ferns and tall old-growth stumps. Then, it dropped down and up a gully before entering the long lane that led steeply down to the barn. Spike, in his position as a slightly elevated member of the human race because of his status as a town kid, was packing my bow and my brand new, store-bought arrow. The cows were strung out about 100 yards ahead of us, and my dad's young prized bull was bringing up the rear. I was wearing my usual oversized rubber boots and my socks had already slid down around my toes.

When Spike pulled and loosed that store-bought arrow, I knew immediately where it was going even though I was 10 feet off to the side. That young bull might have swished his tail, or the arrow might have brushed it to one side, but none of that mattered. The arrow followed the path of a well-placed mortar round and stuck right in his balls, just as I'd known it would even as it left the bow.

Time didn't exactly stand still, but it sure did pause for a minute or two. Long before that hunched up bull got things moving, I had my hot rubber boots churning towards the lane in an effort to cut him off before he started the downhill plunge through the lane to the barn, and to my destruction at the hands of my dad.

The meandering cows were slightly startled as we passed them. The bull beat me to the lane so I launched my boots and myself over the five-wire fence and sprinted down the steep hill, just beating him to the outlet above the barn. The lane was rocky, and he was stumbling as he came towards me. I was trying to decide if I should die at the hands of the bull or my dad when the arrow dropped out and clattered on the rocks.

My dad was always slightly mystified over that bull as he just didn't seem to be a breeder, and once I heard him wondering aloud about the red spot on the rear of the bull's testicles.

THE GOOSE HUNTERS

I must have been eleven because Tige the dog wasn't with us. I think he showed up when I was 12. Once he landed, there were no hunting trips without him. All you had to do was step outside with a shotgun and work the pump and his teeth would start chattering.

It was just Don and Spike and me on this one.

I had started trapping muskrats after school in that river valley below the hill we lived on because there was some stuff I needed to buy. This was western Washington, and the bus ride home from school was long, so the evening trips along the trap line were usually dark, gray, gloomy and rainy. The catching was not that hot either, and I had been scaling down my "to-buy" list, but I was noticing there were lots of ducks and even the occasional flight of geese down there. Killing a goose back then was akin to downing a trophy elk now. There just were not that many of them around.

The Snoqualmie River flooded on a regular basis, and that valley was crisscrossed with drainage ditches. After a flood and before the ditches let the water flow back to the river, you needed to know where to walk as the water could be anywhere from 6 inches to 4 feet deep, and over your head in those ditches.

Don was a country kid like me but from the next valley over and off a raspberry farm, so he was a little more refined than I was. Spike was a town kid. He had thick, tight light brown hair and his nose was too big for the rest of him. He wasn't like the other town kids I knew back then. He was salty, but in a solid, no-bullshit way. He would eventually grow into his nose, but just barely, as he only had eleven more years to live. Another thing we didn't know about him, and that he may also not have known, was that his dad was doing time in the Big House above town. That is what had brought his family there in the first place.

There was slush ice on the floodwater when we crossed the bridge and waded out away from the road in our black rubber knee-boots. We followed the berm left from the ditch dredging and hunted both sides, screened by the cottonwood trees and brush on the berm. As usual, we were wet and freezing because we just did not have enough of or the right kind of clothes, and our socks had slid in those sloppy boots to cover only our toes.

The higher ground of the berm we were on tracked away from the county road for about half a mile, then hooked around to the left back towards the road that continued on toward town, just barely above the floodwater. About 400 yards before reconnecting with the road, the berm petered out and disappeared underwater.

Twice, small flocks of geese had materialized out of the gloom, sailing over while we hissed at each other to "get down" in hopes they would circle to within gun range. We would squat in the squishy, ice-covered mud under the dripping leaves until they disappeared.

We were about halfway out when I killed the first duck. I was shooting my dad's Winchester model 97 twelve-gauge. That is an old pump with a hammer. My hands were so numb I was almost grunting in my effort to pull the trigger. After the duck cartwheeled into the water, I stepped off the berm to retrieve it and went up to my chest in a hole hidden under the floodwater. Now I was really freezing, and the whole safari started going downhill from there.

Don had slipped and gone in over his boots, but not to the extent I had. He had his granddad's twelve-gauge single-shot. That gun was called a Long Tom, and there was a slender steel lever extending back from the receiver towards the small of the stock. You swung it to one side to open the breach. When he finally got a shot the recoil stabbed that lever an inch and a half into his numb frozen hand between his thumb and index finger, and it just stuck there. I was shivering so hard I was of no help but stepped close and watched through a teeth-chattering haze as Spike and Don worked the thing out. It didn't even bleed.

By this point it was getting dark and we were at the end

of the hook. The road home was just over there, and the idea of backtracking for nearly a mile to that road just didn't work because once on the road we still had a half-mile walk to our farm. I was shivering raggedly, and Don was shivering and obsessed with the dark hole in his hand.

Spike made the call. He had not gone in over his boots so was only mildly hypothermic. We would wade across the uncharted waters to the road. Ten yards out we were at the top of our boots and the slush on the water was firming up with the oncoming dark. To this day I don't know how he convinced me to let him get on my shoulders but that is where he ended up riding, carrying both his gun and mine while Don followed carrying the bedraggled ducks and his gun. About half way across I was up to my chest. The slush ice was stacking up against my saturated coat and Spike had been hitching his boots up to keep the water out. That is when the geese dropped out of the low overcast and came right for us, and Spike began frantically hissing for us to "get down."

THE JOCKEY

I was 14 that autumn when the great horserace took place. School was getting started and I had just returned from my first summer job away. My parents had farmed me out as a camp tender for a bunch of uranium prospectors up in the Cascades near Red Mountain. That was the strangest group of people I have ever been associated with up to that time in my life.

The prospectors did not exactly strike it rich and had stiffed me for my summer's wages, so once again I was in search of some quick cash. That is when Pear Shape asked me to help him haul hay to the Washington State Fairgrounds.

Pear, the son of a preacher, had the bad luck to be born with very thin and narrow shoulders, a tiny head and a great big butt. His oversized butt tapered to smallish boots. Somewhere along the way he had adopted the Western mode of dress, and the tight Levi trousers were not a big improvement to his overall looks. When getting on horseback, he would wear a 10-gallon hat and large, batwing chaps. He rented pasture from my parents for his short, stout, black, rough-coated horse, named Ching. Occasionally he would come out, saddle Ching, get his chaps and big hat on and gallop up the steep hill above my parent's house to where he would pose while looking over the valley below. At the age of 14, I had already been in and out of the horse business, so to speak, and would marvel at Ching's ability to carry 300 pounds of Pear, chaps and saddle, at a run up that hill, starting cold.

The way I remember, Pear's social life was somewhat limited, and I imagine his love life was nonexistent, so he was a bit of a clinger when he did hook up with someone. This wasn't my first hay hauling trip with him. He had previously drafted me for a trip down to Portland, Oregon. He was in his mid 30s at the time. I conned my worldly Irish friend, Shane, into going along, and we rode a good part of the way from the Seattle area to Portland on top of the load of hay. I was leaning into the cab of the truck in Portland when Pear jabbed me in the butt with a cattle prod, nearly causing my brain to explode and propelling me clear up onto the seat. Later we found ourselves roaming the darkened residential areas while Pear shined his spotlight into house windows, "looking for an address." Shane had not just fallen off the turnip wagon and allowed as how he knew a pervert when we were sitting next to one. This was news to me, but when you are strapped for cash, strange company is the least of your worries.

There was much more activity than I had expected when Pear and I rolled into the Washington State Fairgrounds with our first load of hay. Livestock and people milled around getting set up for the coming festivities. In addition to being born with an oversized butt, Pear had acquired a big mouth, so it wasn't long before he managed to maneuver himself and Ching into a horserace. The sheriff's posse was on the grounds practicing for the grand entry in a day or two and one of the members, Mr. Butler, was riding the prettiest, most clean-limbed palomino I had ever seen. When I realized what was about to take place, I decided Pear had taken leave of whatever senses he may have possessed to begin with.

The bet was the load of hay we had just hauled against an equivalent amount of money. The distance was a quarter mile, and because Pear was definitely too much of a load for Ching in this high-stakes gamble, a horsey young girl had agreed to ride for him.

If you would have put Mr. Butler and his horse in a local socioeconomic scale of one to 10, they would have been a 10. Pear, Ching and myself, for that matter, would have been about a two, or perhaps a two-point-five, if you were feeling generous.

Word of the impending horserace surged through the grounds and the grandstands quickly filled. The would-be jockey took one look at the really large crowd that had gathered and retired on the spot. When I realized Pear was looking in my direction, I headed for the truck. I had been born with a fully developed case of stagefright, and it had not gotten better in 14 years. As you'll recall, I actually quit Sunday school at the age of six when the church hierarchy fingered me for the role of a shepherd in the Christmas play. I told Pear, in no uncertain words, that I was not going to ride his horse in front of all those people, especially against a horse that would positively disgrace Ching and whoever happened to be on his back.

Those 1950s low-roper Western saddles were never meant for racing. I didn't like them at all. I also didn't like the idea that Pear could only find one of his spurs, but at least it was on my right foot, seeing as I'm right footed. I was absorbing all those handicaps because Pear had dangled $10 cash in front of my nose, to be handed over to me at completion of the race.

Ching figured out what was going on and proceeded to go neurotic. When we came sideways towards the starting line, he at least had all four feet on the ground – from time to time. The starter's handkerchief came abruptly down, and Ching bolted for the finish line. Within a couple of heartbeats I realized we were absolutely running away from Mr. Butler, and evidently he did too because he pulled up. Until that moment I had not realized it, but Ching was a little athlete, a sprinter.

I had jumped the gun, Butler said. At 14 years, most kids in those days were not prone to profanity. I had definitely been behind the starting line when the guy swung his arm because I was looking right at him, so I muttered some of the worst words I had heard to date, being careful Mr. Butler didn't hear me from his elevated position.

The next time we approached the starting line, Ching did it mostly on his back feet with me trying to push his head down. He was positively lathered up and I wasn't doing bad either, plus I was kind of excited, so when the starter dropped his arm I took a viscous swipe at Ching with the spur and missed. The fact he was dancing around on his back legs did not help. Mr. Butler got a good start and just managed to stay ahead of us, me hanging mostly off the saddle because of my stirrup losing jab, and confusing Ching as to what he was supposed to be doing.

Pear, assisted by his big mouth, had a very loud argument with Mr. Butler about the race start. I was resigned, realizing almost instantly that we had just been introduced to that version of the Golden Rule that says those who have the gold make the rules. Adding insult to injury, Pear stiffed me on the $10 plus my hay hauling wages because he was broke.

Waiting for a Sign

TIGE

I must have been about 12 years old when the dog came into my life. There had already been an association with a horse, and even though I have had many associations with horses since, that first one left a bad taste in my mouth.

So when I came trudging up from the school bus stop that spring afternoon in the early 1950s and spied that big yellow dog camped in the hay field below our old house, I didn't just run down there and throw my arms around him. In fact, I squatted down and studied him at least as intently as he was studying me, because it had become clear that you should look a gift horse in the mouth.

My mom had just pulled a fresh batch of bread out of the big wood cook-stove, and she stepped out onto the honeysuckle-wrapped, elevated porch to watch while I took the bread heel as an offering to this newcomer. Already in life I had become a dog man, but was not exactly enamored with our two, Nippy and Wolf. In my opinion, they just were not brash enough.

When I got within ten feet of this lost dog, he growled. More than a growl, it was a rumble coming from somewhere down in his chest. Now this, I thought, is a by-God real dog.

The first thing I did, after naming him Tige and becoming best friends for life with him, was to take him over to my grandparents' place and sic him onto Ranger. That damn Ranger had been whipping Nippy and Wolf for time out of mind, and old Tige tore him up in about two heartbeats. From there we went on to kill skunks, maul porcupines and actually chase the occasional bear. Old Tige was not afraid of man or beast, and that is probably why he could never get his mind around the porcupine enigma. Every time he had a meeting with one he came away looking like a very old, gray-muzzled dog, while the porcupine would stagger off in the other direction, quite a bit lighter, sans quills. Tige would then sit patiently while I pulled quills from his teeth, tongue and jowls. Once, after an historic meeting with one under the porch of the abandoned Armstrong place, I fixed him up. A week or two later I patted him on the nose in passing and something stuck me in the hand. On closer examination I found a quill working its way out through the top of his nose from its starting place in front of his teeth. It slid up easily when I grasped it with a pair of pliers, right out through the top of his rubbery black nose.

Time kind of flew by and before I knew it, I was rolling to town in my '41 Ford and chasing girls instead of chasing varmints with Tige. I was the youngest boy in a family of nine kids, and my parents had most likely wore themselves out raising all them siblings before I came along, so I had always been kind of free on the earth. The trip to town took me across a bridge and down through a river valley below the hill we lived on. As time went by, my return trips eased on into the morning hours, but me and Tige were still best of buddies, because he had taken to chasing the lady dogs of the valley, and more than once I would catch up with him as he loped home on sore feet.

It puts a little lump in my throat now, after all these years, to remember rolling to a stop beside old Tige and opening the offside door. He would climb in and sit on that bench seat next to me. He was a big dog, so our heads were nearly on the same level. There was none of that tail wagging or licking. It was late, and we were serious guys going home.

I remember stopping by the home place on leave from the Marine Corps, and my dad told how Tige had gone off by himself to die. He had dug a little depression under that raised porch and left from there. I was having trouble keeping the moisture confined to my eyeballs as I walked out on that porch and looked down into the hayfield to where I had first seen the old rascal.

Waiting for a Sign

THE ROADSTER

As a 16-year-old wheat-truck driver, I had lots to think about without gawking around, especially coming down off the coulee wall above Grand Coulee Dam with smoking brakes on my way to the granaries at Waterville. But that is what I was doing when I spotted that Model T roadster pickup just down below the road. It was a snapshot thing, and the odds were against my seeing it, but I did see it, and it ended up making a few changes in my fairly fresh life.

The wheat ranch above Grand Coulee was a rite of passage for the boys of my family. My mom had been born on that place to a German steam engineer immigrant who had met and married an Austrian lady immigrant while working the oceangoing ships on the Atlantic route. Why they decided to homestead that scab-rock country is beyond me. My dad had drifted in there horseback from Washington's much greener West Coast, hired on as a teamster driving four horses abreast disking, and the rest is family history.

As the youngest boy-product of that union, I had watched with interest as my older brothers went off from our wet West

Coast farm to that place of summer work, because I knew my time was coming. There were just too many of us, so we were sent over there. Of special interest was the fact they each came home with a deep voice. I thought it probably had something to do with the dry country air.

The only one left of that Germanic tribe when I got there was an old bachelor uncle whose obsession was growing wheat. He was stout, with a prominent nose, one eyebrow that continued from near his left ear to near his right, and with a rare and startling high-pitched laugh.

If I was not telling the story of the roadster, I could tell you more about that place. The high, stark, wooden house stuck up above the surrounding treeless country like a gothic painting, surrounded by low wood outbuildings. The house windows had borders of multicolored glass, and the windmill responded to the constant moaning wind with a slightly out-of-balance thumping.

The logistics of buying the Model T from an old Indian and getting help loading it from the very first black kid I had ever seen (it was a regular United Nations around that place) and then trucking it the 200 miles home to my parent's farm is lost in the fog of time. The summer had produced a bumper crop of wheat, and my uncle gave me a big bonus over and above the normal $300 summer wages. It was a good thing, because building a stock Model T roadster pickup into a fire-breathing street rod was an expensive undertaking, as I was to find out.

The build took place in my dad's recently deceased brother's well-stocked loggers shop, but it didn't happen very quickly. I had a '41 Ford coupe to support, an after-school job in a gas station in town, and girls to chase. At the critical junction where I needed a really good engine, divine providence named Lorne stepped in. Lorne was the premier hot-rodder of the county. He had built up a flathead Ford engine into way more engine than I needed, and why he decided to practically give it to me I'll never know. At that point, he was a wise old guru of nearly 30 years and, I had thought, lived in a parallel but completely separate universe to mine.

After graduating from high school and going totally insane, I went off to Marine Corps boot camp and then infantry training, and the nearly complete roadster sat there on its low-slung wide stance, patiently waiting in the dark oily shop. Before departing for the Far East I turned it over to one of Lorne's contemporaries to finish, and then went and spent my nineteenth birthday on the rolling deck of a troop transport in the South China Sea. One year later, after perusing some of the worst bars that area of the world had to offer from Japan down nearly to Borneo, at taxpayer expense, I came home on leave, accompanied by one of my service buddies.

The roadster was all I had dreamed it would be and then some, and I was slightly euphoric when my friend and I cruised slowly through town on that warm summer evening. We stopped at a crosswalk to let a mother and daughter cross, the roadster pulsing visibly to the tightly harnessed power of that engine. I recognized the girl as the baby sister of a high school acquaintance and asked where he was. The mother smiled thinly as the pretty freckle-faced girl stepped tentatively closer and brought me up to date on her brother's whereabouts. The mother was more prescient than the daughter. If that girl would have had even the slightest touch of the psychic she would have been looking around for a brick to throw at me.

After instilling a sense of dread in my future mother-in-law's breast, and elevating the heart rate of my future wife, we rumbled on through town and turned west onto Highway 2. There was another town down that way, and more people to impress. We were smoking cigarettes with our chins tucked down because this not only looked cool, it kept the easy slipstream from depositing the hot ash on our laps.

My driving career had started very young, driving tractors on my dad's lap at six years and then solo at 13 or thereabouts. I graduated to wheat trucks at 15 and inherited my nearest brother's hopped up '41 Ford coupe at 16 when he went off for Uncle Sam, so I had a feel for rolling stock, and this roadster had a wild feel. It was light, short-coupled and overpowered, and I had absolutely no intention of getting involved in a race that evening, right up until that '54 Mercury came up alongside us on

Highway 2 and would not take no for an answer.

When Highway 2 leaves Monroe going west, it runs a mile or two then makes an easy swing around the Drift-in Tavern and shoots straight as a ruler for quite a few miles, elevated above the low, wet farmlands. The Mercury was a not very attractive two-tone green. I had never seen the guy driving it. We tried to ignore him but he kept surging alongside us, gunning his engine and pointing down the highway. If this would have been a standing start race, a drag race, all he would have seen would have been a cloud of blue-black tire smoke as we left. As it was, we were rolling about 55 miles per hour.

My friend and I gingerly stubbed our cigarettes out on the back tires, which were located just behind our elbows. I studied the rearview mirror and could see a car way back there. He didn't look like a cop, and there was no one coming from the front. I looked over at the guy in the Mercury, pointed down the highway, nodded my head and punched the gas pedal. We shot ahead of him but at 80 miles per hour, I was still trying to make a connection with the roadster so backed off a little, and here he came. I had so much latent power under my right foot I could hardly believe it, but the roadster was feeling as skittish as a neurotic horse. (Recall that I had ridden just such a horse in a grudge race for a too-fat owner at 14 years of age, so knew the feeling).

There was one thing the guy in the Mercury did not know,

and that was we were not going to quit until we went airborne, and probably not even then. We paced him up past 100 miles per hour, then 110, and we were only slightly connected to the highway. At 115 we were running neck and neck with untapped reserves when we heard a thump and his car became enveloped in a cloud of blue smoke. He looked like a smudge fire as he disappeared in the rearview mirror.

We slowed and gradually became more connected to the highway, and then we rolled into the first service station in that next town. I studied the row of Stewart Warner gauges and was relieved to see the little white needles right where they were supposed to be. The cop, that car that was way back there, didn't even bother to turn on his oversized gumball machine. He just stopped his black-and-white behind us and walked up off my left shoulder.

"The first thing I want to know," he said, "is what junkyard you stole this wreck from?"

Those cops, they just have a way with words.

ERRANT MARINE

In 1964, I went to Haiti with an all-volunteer Provisional Marine Air Group to rescue the Americans. Papa Doc was having one of his periodic wars with the Dominican Republic. I doubt the Americans even knew they needed rescuing, but we went anyway. I don't remember if it was going down or coming back, but the assault ship I was on tied up in San Juan, Puerto Rico, and the Marine contingent got shore liberty, but it was Cinderella Liberty, which meant we had to be back aboard by midnight. That was a concept that my friends and I just could not get our minds around.

After a misspent night in the bad bars on the bawdiest side of town, we queued up at about 03:00 and made our way back to the US Naval port. This place was surrounded by an 8-foot high chain-link fence with that barbed wire V on top. Not to worry though, because one of us, a guy named Kesely (only an Irishman would have thought of it) had the foresight to steal an M.P.'s armband, and so lined the six of us up with the intention of marching us through the sentry gate and aboard ship as his faux prisoners. As we neared the gate, the whole thing started looking not really doable to me. I was trailing along in the rear of this motley assembly. Just shy of the gate, I slid into the shadows and watched the whole bunch get arrested, including Kesely and his armband. This left me on the wrong side of the compound with an urgent need to get aboard ship. I had nearly missed a movement in the South China Sea three years earlier, and the military looks askance at those things.

A couple blocks back, I had noticed a palm stump about 4 feet high near the fence, so I backtracked and looked it over from across the street. With a gallon of adrenaline and at least a gallon of cheap booze sloshing through my system, I sprinted across the street, leaped onto the stump, and vaulted into the barbwire V. Leaving a good part of my uniform there, I crashed to the ground on the inside of the fence. At this point, being substantially out of uniform, I couldn't take the usual route up the gangplank (plus it was a little late in the evening for that). The whole place was well-lighted, with walking sentries sprinkled around, and the assault ship looked huge, towering over the quay. Keeping to the shadows, I maneuvered to a Captain's Gig that had been set on the dock. With the nearest sentries going in opposite directions, I scrambled up into the boat, and found myself looking across 6 or 8 feet of space at steel ladder rungs running up to an open elevator. That is when I made the mistake of looking down. Twenty feet below, I could just make out rotten pilings and oily black water.

There it was....decision time. I could get arrested, or take the leap. I took the leap, scurried up the ladder and found myself on the hangar deck.

Assault ships are bigger than you would think, and it took me the better part of an hour to find our compartment. Along the way, I got some funny looks from the sailors due to my scattered uniform and dripping blood. All would have been well, but I got into the compartment just as the guys were rolling out for morning calisthenics. After describing my heroic boarding to a strangely silent audience, I turned around to find the Gunny standing behind me. Luckily, he was my fishing partner, and I only received a one-hour tongue lashing. Kesely and his ensemble got into big trouble.

Waiting for a Sign

THE SALMON FISHERMEN

We were not aware of it, but it was a very serious case of the blind leading the blind. We were in an insufficient boat, crossing the Columbia River Bar in a thick early morning fog, headed for the salmon fishing grounds straight out into the Pacific Ocean. All we did was follow the commercial boats because we assumed they knew where they were going. We were going out there because that is where the salmon were. It was like the convicted bank robber replying to the reporter who asked why he robbed banks, and the con replied, "Because that is where the money is."

We were young and we were salty, ex-Navy and ex-Marine, and we had seen the Elephant and heard the Owl, so to speak. Up until that morning, I had assumed the Columbia River Bar was a beer joint somewhere down on the Columbia River. I was completely oblivious to the fact that this was where the mighty Columbia River meets the Pacific Ocean, and that it is one of the most dangerous places in the world for an uninformed boater.

Trouble starts there when the Columbia River current rides out into the Pacific, but the Pacific tide wants to push it back up the Columbia, and then this big wind coming out of the Columbia River Gorge gets involved. In this case, the bar was flat going out, only because conditions were exactly right. Once we were in the ocean proper, it began those long breaths under us and we started riding the waves and troughs. If you were prone to sea sickness, this is where it would get you. One minute you would be up, seeing boats vaguely through the fog, and the next moment you are down, seeing no one.

The boat we were in should never have been allowed anywhere near the saltwater, or freshwater, for that matter. It belonged to my friend Tom, who, I had already decided, would rather fish than chase girls. The condition of the boat did not even enter into his sphere of awareness. It could have been covered with stainless steel or rust. That didn't matter. What mattered was getting to the fish. This one was boxy and old, made out of spongy plywood, with two mismatched outboard motors. The life vests were as old as the boat, also spongy, and probably would not float. And, this boat leaked.

When you fish in the ocean for salmon, you look for a concentration of boats. We got in the middle of them, shut the motors off and started jigging, and the water started coming inside the boat. Soon it was up around our shoes, so we fired up the motors, ran the boat up on plane and pulled the plug in the back and drained the water out. Then we circled back into the concentration of boats, and that is when we got into the salmon.

Catching salmon can do some funny things to your mind. They are big and wild. The boat is heaving to the belly swells of the ocean, and you are in the middle of a school. Reeling in and netting 10 and 15 pound Cohos, dragging them over the side and killing them with a leaded club is intoxicating, and you can certainly lose track of how deep the water has become in the bottom of the boat. And that is just what we did.

When the lull in the catching hit, I think we all looked down at the same time and all noticed that the water was clear up around our ankles.

With both motors running wide open, we could only just wallow, up one side of the big ocean swells, and down the other. We were too full of water and there was no getting up on plane. We were sinking and the water in that place is very cold, even in the summer. Bailing was frantic, using emptied lure boxes and beer mugs. Slowly, and I mean very slowly, the boat picked up speed and we were finally able to get on plane and pull the plug and watch all that water run out the back and return to the ocean.

The bar was making up a little when we came in so we rode up and down the sides of 6 to 8-foot swells, but they were not breaking. It was one of those deals where that God that watches over a boatload of idiots just happened to be on duty, so we cruised on around the jetty and tied up to the dock. After all that strenuous work, we needed hamburgers, and lots of beers.

We were a raucous little group when we left the eatery with the intention of loading the boat and starting the long drive home. But, silence prevailed when we discovered the boat had sunk, right there at the dock. It was hanging by guitar string tight mooring lines, and it was mostly underwater.

"The Aviator"

Brady on the right, Cole on the left about the age when Brady flew off the roof with his home made wings.

Brady flying for the Army in Vietnam.

"The Jockey"

Working as a camp tender for the uranium prospectors about a month before Cole rode in the horse race.

"Tige"

The 41 Ford.

"The Roadster"

Finally complete.

"Errant Marine"

Above: Cole as a U.S. Marine.

Left: With the Seventh Fleet in the South China Sea, on the beach of Mindoro.

"The Salmon Fishermen"

Tom & his leaky boat.

Fishing out of the mouth of the Columbia. Cole, right.

"Stoney" and "Guillotine"

Cole's Family, left to right: Justin, Cole, Carol and Louie Smith.

"The Gourmet Cook"

Working south of Jackson Hole, Wyoming.

"The Neophyte"

Working as a cold weather cowboy.

"The Aerobats"

Left: Cole, during the time of hangar construction.

Below: Cole sitting on the wing of his own little commuter aircraft.

Waiting for a Sign

THE NEOPHYTE

In 1977, at the ripe age of 35, I decided on a career adjustment, so to speak. As a moderately successful West Coast businessman with a young family and all the stuff, including a slightly out-of-hand drinking problem, a change of scenery seemed in order. Actually, regular trips to AA would have been a lot less dramatic than the route I chose.

The interview with the old rancher at the big ranch in north-central Wyoming went something like this:

"Are you a cowboy?"

Me: "No."

"Are you an irrigator?"

Me: "Noo."

" Farmer?"

"Nooo, but I can fly an airplane." (I had seen a landing strip on the way to the ranch office).

Blank stare from the old guy.

"Just what can you do?" he asked, and in a slightly panicked state, I smoothly suggested I had never found anything I couldn't do.

"Now that, by God, is the way I have always felt about life," the old guy said.

So there we were, deposited in the hired-hand house, my wife with our five-week old boy on her hip, and our five-year-old son dancing around the yard in the middle of rattlesnake country in July.

Thirty-five years is a little late in life for this kind of change, and I remember slight tremors from my liver, going from a thrice weekly drenching to six months without even seeing a town, let alone a cocktail lounge.

The summer was taken up with irrigating interspaced with stacking thousands of bales of hay while running the self-propelled stacker, all while my brand-new saddle hung in the garage gathering dust.

I had not let on at the interview but I had been on horseback off and on from the time I was a little kid. It was a good thing I hadn't let on. Working horseback along the Big Horn Mountains in Wyoming is not related in any way to the kind of riding most people have ever done, and the fact you have ridden a few horses has nothing whatsoever to do with being a cowboy.

We went mostly at a trot, for eight to twelve-hour days. The owner had suggested I throw my shiny new saddle in the creek for the night, and then ride it wet, something I could not bring myself to do, and so paid the price with twisted knees and pigeon-pointed toes.

With very little warm-up, I found myself trailing "the gather" down country while my day boss cleaned that giant pasture and brought them to me. He rode a leggy dappled gray and kept a shot whip coiled on his saddle near his rope. Everything looked tight and functional. Two blue heelers worked with him. I remember one was named Gus. He would dive off the right-side canyon and disappear into the creek, only to reappear up the other side, where he would pick up a bunch of cow/calf pairs and bring them to me through the canyon bottom.

After this had become slightly routine, I watched him come down the other side with about 15 pairs and disappear, but he did not come up. In a little bit, Gus came up and went home, along with the other dog. When he still did not come up, I eased away from the gather and rode over for a peek. He and his bunch were having a fight about crossing the creek and he had his whip down. (I found out later this was what Gus took as his signal to head for home.) He spotted me gawking over the edge and charged up to refresh my memory as to my job. What I was supposed to be doing was to keep the gather moving down the country, and he would take care of cleaning the pasture.

So, on we went, and after a bit he stalled out down there again, and I just kept my horse and that growing bunch of cows and calves trundling along. Shortly, here he came. His gray horse was lathered up, and his whip was trailing in the grass when he slid to a stop about a foot from me, stared me in the eye and allowed, "A man could die down in that creek bottom and old Cole Smith would not care. No sir, he would just keep moseying down country."

Here all this time I had thought being a drunk and running a business had been confusing.

THE GUILLOTINE

After leaving the big ranch, my life took a couple of twists and turns, and then my little family and I ended up buying the Little Canyon Creek Ranch just downstream from Big Trails. It was not exactly "The Grapes of Wrath" all over again; that would come later.

When you are on one of those little hard-luck cow/calf operations, you work with your neighbors and so, the deal was I would load up in the dark with my neighbor to try to salvage their early spring calving operation.

They had been calving on an old ground. It was a rainy and snowy spring, and scours was rampant, so they had decided to jump the gun and take the whole herd off the contaminated grounds and out to their spring grass in the badlands.

I remember it was dark and raining lightly when my guy backed up to my new loading chute in his 1-ton truck. The truck had a guillotine gate, and I started leading my horse up the ramp, only to have him hang the saddle horn up on a crosspiece in the chute. Unsaddling, I led him in and resaddled in the dark, wondering if I had included any part of the truck in the cinch. It was still dark and raining when we got to the assembly point in the badlands, just north and east of Buffalo Creek. After hoisting the gate, I coached my horse to the back where he stalled, and, thinking back, I can hardly fault him. It was gloomy and dark gray, he was standing on some slippery boards, and I was asking him to take a leap of faith out into the void. When he did jump, he jumped up and out, which was not a real good idea. The saddle horn caught on the guillotine gate and jerked my horse into a back flip out into the dark and gooey badlands mud. It also broke my saddle horn.

Before I got mixed up in this cowboy/rancher stuff, I had done a lot of afternoon business in the cocktail lounges on the West Coast. I had especially liked the piano bars. At an early time of the afternoon those places were usually mostly deserted, and there would be some dreamy-eyed, just past her prime lady playing easy music while the place kind of enveloped you, quietly brushing away your cares. Leaning an elbow on the piano and humming along was encouraged, and if you could sing, so much the better. This was all good clean fun, and all of us drunks were well dressed and clean. And, strangely enough, by late afternoon, all of us could sing. So of course, I went off to Wyoming.

Up till now, this had not been a real good day. Then things got a lot worse. Buffalo Creek was over the banks with the runoff.

We had cows and scoured calves. We had pregnant cows. It was raining and snowing. We needed to get across Buffalo Creek, and the ground on both sides had turned to jelly. We pushed little bunches in. The banks were steep, the creek was deep, and they started bogging. In the movies, you just drop a loop on a bogged cow and spur your horse a little and drag her out. In real life, that is not even close. When one bogs, you get off and slog over with your catch rope, work it around her girth and stuff the bitter end out between her front legs. We did that. We three, (there was other help) dallied on our saddle horn – remember, mine was broken – and then we spurred. My horse was stout and walked ahead like a tractor hooked to an unmovable object. Then he just went up and up, and because of my broken saddle horn and pinched dally, over backwards, right down into Buffalo Creek, upside down.

This was not my first rodeo, so to speak, but I had never had a horse land partway on top of me and drive me down into a chocolate milkshake, which was the consistency and temperature of Buffalo Creek during the spring runoff. It is not a good feeling to be squirming around down there, but what really caused me to reevaluate the cowboy life was when we took a noon break. I fished my good sandwich out of my saddlebag, and it dripped between my fingers like the badlands mud it had become. And then, I remembered the piano bars.

Waiting for a Sign

STONEY

In the mid-1980s, my wife, our two boys and I owned the most beautiful little Wyoming ranch I had ever imagined. In an effort to alleviate the starving there, I was constantly working to make the place more productive.

There was a red sandstone shelf that obstructed the development of a road to the last field going down the creek, so I had determined to blast it out of the way. That is where John Stoneman came into the picture. In Washakie County, John Stoneman was known simply as "Stoney, "and that name was apt. He was a Pennsylvania Dutchman capable of anything and everything. To shake hands with him was seriously like grasping a chunk of granite. In profile, with his jutting beard and hooked nose, he looked like an Old Testament patriarch, but was much thicker. His arms were like the proverbial oak tree. And, he was a dynamiter.

Drilling and shooting red sandstone is a real pain in the butt. It is fractured, so the drill is constantly getting stuck in the layers. I was using a fertilizer and diesel mixture in the holes and pushing a Tovix sausage in on top, then tying it to the other holes with det. cord and setting the whole thing off with an electric cap. About three-quarters of the way through the shelf, I ran out of det. cord, and, as it turned out, Stoney, my appropriately licensed supplier, was also out of it.

It was midwinter in Wyoming. That is when the temperature can nosedive to 40 below without warning. Stoney had a source for more blasting material and had a '65 Nash Rambler we would drive to get the stuff. We only had to cross Powder River Pass's extremely icy summit at 9,660 feet above sea level at night, and then brave the frigid plains out east of Buffalo, that area where all the English cowmen's dreams had died in the blizzard of 1889.

The heater in Stoney's Rambler didn't work, but I had been forewarned, so I had on most of the clothes I owned plus I had a black knit navy watch cap on my head, as did Stoney. Stoney was a Mason and devout Christian, and I was tinkering with Buddhism, so our conversation was fragmented. Plus, I had an abscessed tooth that was driving me crazy in that cold clammy car.

When we rolled into Buffalo, Stoney maneuvered into the drive-in window of the very first liquor store, and I bought a bottle of brandy to alleviate the pain in my jaw, and just to be safe, I bought a second one.

I believe there are still fragments of our old tribal

affiliations. When Stoney and I crunched through the gravel on that frigid moonlit night and stopped in front of the trailer office of the oilfield explosives, I could see, through my brandy-and-throbbing-toothache-induced haze, an instant and lasting connection between Stoney and the watchman that ran the place. They were explosives men.

After they filled the trunk with det. cord and electric caps, I passed one of the brandy bottles out the window, and Stoney and his tribesman got down to business. There were explosives that had been weather damaged on the jobs and could no longer be used in the oil fields, so they filled the back seat. Then, because these two guys were so happy to have reconnected after who-knows-how-many centuries, they filled the space under my feet until I was looking between my knees out the windshield.

By the time we had regained the summit of Powder River Pass, the brandy had bridged the gap between rigid Christianity and some pretty loose Buddhism. We were connected. We understood how the entire universe worked and had always worked.

I had been looking at Stoney off and on during this safari because he was a singular looking guy with his watch cap, hooked nose and beard. He had piercing eyes under that black knit cap. He looked exactly like I imagined a 1980s terrorist would look, sitting on enough explosives to blow a good part of Wyoming right off the map. I was ruminating on just how a

Wyoming state trooper might address this scene when Stoney lost control of that explosive-laden Rambler.

It is amazing how quickly a toothache will go away when you are tracing a slow S path down off a mountain in an explosive laden car in the cold early morning hours. When we got stopped, we were sideways to the universe, and very quiet.

Our philosophical discussion had gone cold, and Stoney allowed as how we had better get down off the mountain.

HORSEBACK ON A FROSTY MORNING

It was in late fall, 1994 or 5. Jonsey and I unloaded up above Deer Haven, a lodge on the west side of the Big Horn Mountains in north-central Wyoming. From there we rode through a mile of timber to start gathering cattle off the big mountain meadows and on towards the mountain cabin. Jonsey had a spare horse with him that trailed along. A family of blue grouse jumpstarted my horse's heart and, by extension, mine. The high, clear mountain air was nearly as intoxicating as a six pack of good beer.

Our boss and another guy had hauled up to the cabin, and then ridden across to help. By evening we had the pasture cleaned of about 700 pairs, dropped the cows and calves through a gate, and rode back up to the cabin. The ground was frozen, but the weather looked good when we turned the horses into the corral and hung all our saddles and tack on the rails. As we drove down through Brokenback, the plan for the next morning changed, with Jonsey and the other guy bringing new horses and gathering up through a chunk of ground south of the cabin, while the boss and I retrieved the horses at the cabin, met up with Jonsey at the drop point, and everyone continued off the mountain with the cows.

There was four inches of snow on my saddle next morning when we caught the horses. Snow was frozen to their backs, and scratching it off with the curry comb had my horse pretty well wired up by the time I got the saddle on him. I had a halter and lead on one of the spare horses, and two were going to run loose. All of them were milling in the corral, blowing steam into the cold morning, and I was getting an uneasy feeling about this safari. The boss had all the rails down except one and was eying his green horse with a speculative air.

A cut ran up hill from the cabin and through some timber to hit the open ground. The plan was to get in front of the loose horses in the confines of the cut and get them settled down, so when we broke on top we could all amble towards the cows, about a mile or two away to the west. When I climbed aboard, my young Morgan gelding felt goosier than I had on my first date. The fact he was barefoot didn't exactly elevate my confidence. The boss dropped the last rail, stepped into the saddle, and informed me he thought his horse was going to buck and that I shouldn't let the loose horses get past me.

We were all crowded up and milling sideways towards the start of the cut when his horse loudly broke wind and bucked off into the timber. That was the starting gun, with both loose horses lunging to pass me on the left, and the haltered one on the

74

right. We were neck and neck as we rocketed the 500 feet up the cut and turned in tight formation towards the west.

That ground fell away, and was broken with islands of scrub evergreens and old blow-downs. Even as we thundered into the open I knew the race was lost, but my young Morgan didn't. Each time we jumped a sage brush or downed tree, the lead rope stretched my right arm like a rubber band. The barefoot horse on snowy, frozen ground felt like he was running on a sloped floor of ball bearings. My heart was six inches into my throat and beating my tonsils silly. Applying the brakes, while watching those two loose delinquents gallop off into the distance, was a long and sensitive process.

We were stopped a half mile from the cut with huge puffs of frozen breath spiraling upwards. Both horses were also breathing hard. I was trying to pry the lead rope from my cramped frozen fingers when the boss rode up and observed that, as far as he was concerned, "There is nothing to compare with being horseback on a frosty morning."

Waiting for a Sign

THE ACROBATS

I guess it must have been sometime in the 90s. I had contracted to build a big custom airplane hangar complex for a wealthy ex-restaurateur who also happened to be an airplane nut. This job was in northern Colorado, so I would be staying down there. To save money, I moved a camper trailer onto the jobsite, driving back to my home near Ten Sleep on the weekends.

As it turned out, the guy I was building for was in his 70s, divorced, estranged from his family on the East Coast, and lonely. He was also an ex-Air Force flying officer, ex-aerobatics competitor, and had a loose grip on a short temper.

Once the project was underway, he began stopping by my trailer in the evening and suggesting we take one of his three aircraft out for a spin. At that point, I had been a licensed pilot for about 30 years, but for you non-pilots, there are licensed pilots, and then there are real pilots. This guy was a real pilot.

He gave me a crash course in landing and taking off his Bird Dog, Cessna's last military tail dragger, and then we moved on up to the RV-4. This is a little low-wing, tandem-seat, hot-rod capable of most aerobatic maneuvers (in the hands of a competent pilot) that you actually kind of wear instead of sitting in.

It was fall, and the weather had cooled, so when we taxied out that evening, the bubble canopy quickly fogged from my overheated body, brought on by my overheated imagination (this was not my first flight with this guy). My self-appointed instructor was in the front seat with his 1950s Air Force helmet on. It said "Blue Dog" on the back. The radio was not working properly, nor was the intercom. When we stopped at the runway threshold, I reached up to wipe some of the condensation off the canopy so I could at least see if there was any traffic coming downwind, but was quickly admonished by Blue not to scratch the canopy. He kept bending over and fiddling with something under the instrument panel and finally jerked his helmet off, handed it over the seat to me and took my headset. I plopped the helmet on and plugged in when Blue yelled, over the engine noise, with no intercom, that to hell with it, he was taking off. There was a sliver of clear windscreen in front of him from the underwhelming defroster. Everything else was like looking out from the inside of a jar full of milk.

This little airplane, with the throttle firewalled, climbed briskly in the cool evening air. Blue was flying still bent over messing with the intercom plugs, so I surreptitiously wiped a clear spot on the canopy (I hate the thought of a midair collision) and that is when I missed the "signal." There are two ways of passing control in a tandem-seat airplane. You can agree, over the intercom, to pass control, or, sans the intercom, you vigorously shake the stick. Blue, intent on fixing the intercom and radio, passed control by shaking the stick while I was busy wiping a spot on the canopy so I could see if we were sharing this airspace with anyone else.

Without getting technical, this airplane was trimmed for takeoff (climb), the throttle was up against the wall, Blue was trying to fix the radio, and I was looking out from under his cockeyed helmet trying to see out the window. The only one flying was the aerodynamics. It climbed until it ran out of airspeed, then a portion of the left wing kind of stalled so it rolled on its side, and the nose described a fairly abrupt downward arc and...

I had been having some business problems on another project, not related to Blue's, so I was kind of preoccupied but in the back of my mind I was thinking, "Come on Blue, we don't need to get this fancy." Once the airplane was pointed at the ground, it of course got going very fast, (remember, the engine is still in climb mode), the wings started generating lift, and up we went, again. Up, up and up until it ran out of airspeed and rolled on its side, and down we went again. I had been on the verge of a solution to my business problem, but it is hard to hold a thought when your stomach is hanging 5,000 feet in the air, and a lousy-fitting old Air Force helmet keeps sliding over your eyes.

After the third trip down, I noticed we were getting closer to the ground (the canopy was clearing) each time we hit the bottom of this arc and was about to mention this to Blue when he straightened up and yelled, "You're getting too close to Boulder," whereupon I lost all interest in business problems and grabbed the stick with both hands (and they immediately became sweaty).

My body and mind cooled as I flew a standard pattern (Blue actually landed it – insurance considerations), and then I taxied over to his rented hangar.

After swinging the tail smartly around in front of the hangar and shutting down, I dismounted. Blue fiddled with the radio for a minute, then climbed out and demanded to know what the hell kind of maneuvers I had been doing up there. I apologized for being too engrossed in my business problems to do a reasonable job of flying and aimed my shaky legs towards my trailer.

THE TEAM ROPER

I think it was about 1991, and we were back in Ten Sleep. After a long day piloting my 1957 John Deere paddlewheel scraper back and forth through the little gully on the west end of my farm ground in an effort to build an irrigation pond – a task similar to driving a large wood cooking range around on a hot summer afternoon – I happened to see dust rising from the Ten Sleep rodeo grounds. Needing very little reason to quit, I wandered over to the arena.

John Jones and the Hyattsville crew were doing a little not-too-serious team roping. I sidled up to the fence and got a view between the rails. Not wanting to interrupt the proceedings, I was conscious of where I positioned myself, and got to watch a few good runs. I knew these guys vaguely from my previous stay in the Ten Sleep area, so was aware this wasn't the first time they had done this. I noticed they each had a spare horse or two tied out of the way, and saw them occasionally switch mounts, so guessed this was also a training session for the rope horses.

It was hot and dusty. After my day on the scraper, I was wishing I had a cold beer to wash my throat. My baseball hat was pulled low to keep the afternoon sun out of my eyes, and I was enjoying the spectacle as an anonymous and even unnoticed observer.

That's when Jonsey rode over to me. I had provided him with some horse pasture seven or eight years before, and had drunk a few beers with him in the Ten Sleep bars. He inquired if I had ever done any roping when I had that place up at Big Trails, just down the creek from Ped Miles. Like an idiot, I said yeah, when I had a sick cow, or a calf with the scours. I forgot to mention that most of this had been done from the back of a pickup truck.

So the deal was I had my choice. I could head one or heel it on a really tall, orange-ticked white horse that he provided. When I climbed aboard, the first thing I noticed was the stirrups were about an inch too long. I had to reach for them with the toes of my boots. Things had gone quiet in the arena, and I knew I was about to be the star attraction. Even though I willed it not to, my mind was already beginning to slip into neutral. About then I mumbled something to Jonsey about not having been horseback for eight years. Being the gentleman he is, Jonsey suggested he head, to save me from total embarrassment, I am sure. Since my brain was already in neutral, I mentioned I didn't think I could catch one by the heels, but was sure I could catch one by the head. Hoo boy...

After backing the big horse into the left box, I began

sorting the rope coils and the reins, all the while reaching for the stirrups with my toes. Jonsey, in the right box, quietly suggested I grip the horn to help keep my seat on the jump out of the box. Having already filled my left hand with the coils and reins, the horn hardly fit. Catching Jonsey grinning, I quickly switched hands. Those other guys, and one woman, were paying more attention than they probably had to anything since their first lecture on the difference between boys and girls in sixth grade health class.

It seems the header is the trigger man. All you have to do is nod your head, and total chaos ensues. The chute clanged, and that big, sleepy white horse jumped three-quarters of the way out from under me. Within one second he was running harder than any horse I had ever been on. I was sitting up on the cantle, with fourteen-and-a-half inches of saddle between me and the horn. The stirrups were hanging upside down from my toes. The pre-nod nervous sweat was partially blinding me.

By the time I had slipped back down where I belonged, there were dirt clods as big as baseballs flying by my head from the horse and steer's hooves. Swinging the loop was a battle against the G-forces imposed on me by the fast-running horse. It was with total amazement that I saw the loop settle over the offside horn and the steer's nose. The relief was complete.

But something in the back of my mind was nudging me as I looked down at that quick running steer with the loop on his nose and horn.

"There is one more thing you have to do," my subconscious seemed to be saying.

Just then is when the orange-ticked white horse took a left. Without a dally, and with a foot of slack in the rope, the steer just does not follow. In fact, he kept going straight ahead. Of course, when the first two coils smoked through my right hand, I instinctively gripped the rope harder. That was enough to lever me up and out of the saddle, setting me up for a swan dive into the north end of the arena. Mercifully, the tension jerked the steer's nose up, and the loop slipped off, just as I caught myself with the toe of my left boot jammed into the horse's girth.

Since, I have noticed that when ropers ride back down the arena they frequently look thoughtful as they coil their ropes. Although my rope was dragging, I think I might have looked like that as I studied the shiny half inch smoking groove through the palm of my right hand. The rabid clapping from the gallery unsettled me, and I may have been less than appreciative when they invited me to rope with them "anytime."

THE GOURMET COOK

There was a rich guy south and east of Jackson Hole that wanted me to build a big indoor riding arena for him, with an attached stable area. I needed the work so pursued it, but could not get the guy off-center. Summers are short in Wyoming, especially in that area. We were still dithering around when August showed up, and I was ready to walk away from the project when the guy suddenly gave us the go ahead.

Putting a crew together for that remote place was not easy, and with the construction-stopping winter staring me in the face, I enlisted Stoneman. That is the same Stoney of dynamite fame from an earlier story. At that point in our lives we were neither of us young men. In fact, my fiftieth birthday was a vague memory, and I suspect Stoney's sixtieth might have been just as vague for him.

We moved a smallish camp trailer onto the site, conned a young, tough guy named Johnnie to help, and went to work. The building would be huge, 100 feet wide by 260 feet long, with an attached 40 foot wide by 200 foot long stable area. First we did the site grading, then the massive footings with a rebar plan that would have confused a Chinese Mensa member.

By the second day of concrete work my hands were cracked and bleeding, but we could actually feel the temperature dropping so scurried ahead. The routine was to get out of the trailer by 5 a.m. and get working, in the dark, after downing a cup of tea or coffee. There was no stopping for lunch as Stoneman was positive a lunch made a person doggy and less productive, and to work with him doing concrete was a humbling and awe-inspiring experience so I assumed he was correct. At 5 p.m., if we did not have concrete trucks onsite, we would load up in the pickup and travel east for a mile in the dusky evening to the Elk Horn Trading Post to shower. There was a bar and one shower stall, so two of us would drink beer while the third showered, then we would rotate.

With stomachs shrunk to the size of ping-pong balls, the beer and fatigue would get right to work, and we were wooden when we returned to the trailer to start supper. Stoney was a meat, potatoes and cabbage guy and a tyrant in the kitchen, and in his mind, there could never be too much garlic.

In the beginning, supper was an enormous affair, and there were times I thought I could hear stomachs stretching. Soon, we decided the beer we were consuming at the Elk Horn was just not enough to get us through the evening so took to bringing two jumbo beers each home. After that, supper was an enormous and riotous affair, with much discussion of the merits of garlic in the cooking. With the cold outside increasing, the moist propane cooking and heating burners added to the coziness, as did the smell of our work clothes, work boots, work socks, and, later in the restless night, the partially digested cabbage and garlic.

The Mexican steel workers and the prefabricated building package came on site with the first snowstorm. The Herculean effort on the concrete work was paying off, with the vertical steel setting down over our very large structural bolts like the exact jigsaw puzzle they were. We wrapped up on Christmas Eve. Stoney was making the last of the welds from the inside of a badly fogged welding helmet at 20 below zero while I lay on my back in the slow-blowing snow under our work trailer trying to figure out why the lights and my fingers had all quit working.

As we crawled up and over a snowy Togwotee Pass in the dark, with a blacked out work trailer shadowing us en-route to Ten Sleep and home, Stoney confided in me that he had not slept well the whole four months, and he also confessed his stomach had never felt well the entire time. This seemed a mystery to him, considering how hard we had worked.

Waiting for a Sign

COW DOGS

It was spring 1993. The south side of the barn was gathering heat all day and radiating it out in the night, so the snow was melted at least ten feet out, and there were even patches of dry red dirt on that side of the barn. After a long winter, it made you just want to sit there and contemplate the clear blue sky and maybe spit and whittle some.

I had volunteered to help John Jones trail his herd across the badlands to his allotment on the Gooseberry.

No sooner had I saddled my horse than winter returned, and when Jonsey showed up that morning at the old Ten Sleep beet dump, I was hanging around with two inches of wet snow on my saddle looking at a fresh-born calf. Jonsey allowed as how there were a few late calvers in the bunch, so we dropped her and headed west.

Jonsey had two working dogs at that time, Baldy and Red. Baldy was a chunky border collie, and Red was a red-ticked heeler. These were busy dogs, and they loved to chase rabbits. That spring the badlands were absolutely full of rabbits. We hadn't topped the hill above the dump when I heard Jonsey bellow the first of the days refrain, "Baldy, Red, Gawd-damn you, get back here!"

The new snow was melting fast, and the cows were churning up the gooey badland mud. Soon it was so deep udders were dragging, and calves attempting to grab a sip on the go were slobbering in disappointment. Baldy's tail was also down and dragging in the mud, and probably weighed ten pounds all by itself. Their rabbit chasing had slowed dramatically, but was still in effect to the point that Jonsey had to frequently repeat his admonition. About 10 a.m., a cow pulled off to the side and birthed a calf. We would come back and load those two up after settling the herd for the night.

We took turns going back and getting the pickup and horse trailer, driving up the old road a few miles past the bunch to leave it, and then coming back to push them along. About noon an amazing thing happened. I had ridden back, loaded up, and drove past the outfit and on down the road four or five miles. There I unloaded and, after riding back for an hour, was surprised I hadn't found them. I rode to the highest hill in the area, and looked carefully at a hundred thousand acres, but saw nothing. It was as if they had disappeared from the face of the earth. For a fraction of a second I wondered if they had all been "taken up."

This was a little disconcerting, and of course my mind immediately started malfunctioning. Had we been on the north side of the road, I wondered? (I knew better). After trotting off that way for a mile, I reversed course and was soon loping in the other direction for another mile. My horse commenced getting lonely too, and began calling long and loud for his buddy. I would probably still be out there galloping in unorganized circles had Jonsey not awakened from his siesta and walked out to skylight on the edge of the bowl they had stopped in.

Things were drying out some when we rousted them and continued. By the time we dropped the bunch for the night, most of the clinging mud had worn off Baldy's tail and Red's feet, and the rabbits were under siege again, with Jonsey railing on the dogs to "get back here."

It was evening when we pulled up to the cow with her newborn, and right away I could tell she didn't want any company. After strategically placing the trailer, and stringing the panels from the side, Jonsey looked the situation over with a practiced eye, and allowed as fact that this cow was not going to like those two dogs hanging around. We opened the little door in the gooseneck, hoisted them up and slammed them in. At that point, I decided the most constructive thing I could do was get out of the way, so I sat off to one side on my horse, looking important to any uninformed passerby, (in the badlands?) and watched Jonsey do what he does best. After performing some cowman magic, he had the cow and calf in the front of the trailer, our horses in the back half, and the panels replaced on the side.

As we walked towards the cab, Jonsey stopped, exasperated and muttered "Those dam dogs are gone again," and then, looking out at the huge expanse of badlands, yelled, "Baldy, Red, Gawd-damn you, get back here!"

I looked up at the little window in the gooseneck to see his two devoted helpers staring out with cocked heads and lolling tongues.

THE HORSE PACKER

In October 2008, my son Louie and I were helping the local outfitter with two elk hunting clients from Pennsylvania, a dad and a son. The dad had killed his bull, and was hanging around while Lou took the boy out to get his. After about a week, Lou decided to take the kid into the "Honey Hole." This is a place up in the Bighorns where the elk go to hide after they have been shot at. There is no trail into that place. It is a secret spot.

So the deal was, I would ride my saddle horse, Bud, lead a packhorse with the abbreviated spike camp on it, Lou and the kid would share a horse by walking and riding, and the dad, to stave off boredom, would ride in and out with me on Goldie.

There was five inches of snow on the ground when we looked furtively around and slipped off the Lost Twin trail and into the steep timber. If you screw up on this trip, you end up in the blow-down timber and rock faces. As we went up, I knew we were not tracking correctly, but did manage to hit the critical spots to get through below the rock walls and eventually end up above timber line and in the correct meadow. It is a chancy thing.

The snow in these high meadows was cut up with elk tracks. We found the secret spot, brushed snow aside and set up the tent, pumped water through the purifier from a nearby pothole, and then gathered up the horses for the trip off the mountain. This would leave Lou and his client free to hunt afoot, while the dad and I rode off the mountain, me leading the extra horses.

The trip up had been harder than previous ones, so in my mind, I was searching for the mistakes I had made. As we started down, I followed our tracks in the snow. This is steep country, heavy with timber, cut up with blow-down and rock faces. After slipping and sliding for about half an hour, following our previous track, I decided to bear off to the left to avoid a particularly nasty spot, planning to bear right and pick up our trail down a ways. Once around the bad spot I eased right. Then I eased right some more, crossing our trail in a snow-free spot, unbeknownst. Soon, things started looking funny. Even the watery sun looked in the wrong place. The snow under the trees was untracked, the blow-down thicker, the ground steeper and the rock faces were closing in. That is when my usually razor-sharp mind started malfunctioning. If the trail was to my right, why was the setting sun, watery as a store-bought egg, over my left shoulder, when it should have been slightly over my right one? And why had I led this guy from Pennsylvania into this steep, slippery place when he was not any kind of a horseman. I looked back and noted he

94

had lost his lucky hunting hat. It was one of those 1920-type tan things with the tiny bill and rolled-up sides.

Your mind can do funny things if you let it. With my horses practically sitting down and sliding on their butts, I almost let go my grip. We were really in the wrong place.

Then, we dropped out of the timber into a meadow and onto a deep, well-worn trail, and it should not have been there. My mind went totally blank. If we had not crossed our trail, we should have been left of it, but the sun, what there was of it, should have been slightly in front of my right shoulder, but was somewhere over my left shoulder, so…

I turned right onto the trail, and, leading my horses, trotted up the trail, completely befuddled. That is when my guy, faithfully following on Goldie, shouted up that the trailhead was just down to our left a mile. I told him that of course, I was aware of that and just wanted to look at something on the trail. And then, almost magically, I managed to swing the whole earth 180 degrees and realign it to conform to my new heading.

WAITING FOR A SIGN

RUNNING HORSES

It was in the fall when I got a call. My sixtieth birthday was a very vague memory. A lady rancher needed some help getting her horse herd onto winter pasture. My son Louie and I went over. There were about 18 head of mares. The ranch lady gave us instructions before we climbed aboard our horses, and the instructions were pretty vague. She was riding a really long-legged, Roman-nosed quarter horse that looked like it could run. I saw her give Bud and Goldie – our Morgan horses — a cursory glance. She was not impressed. Her brother was going to go up ahead of us on a four-wheeler to get the gates open.

She took a head start to run up a ways, and then Lou and I let the mares out the gate. They went out at a gallop, took an immediate hard left and then side-hilled down into a creek bottom. There were about four inches of fresh fall snow on mud.

If you have never run horses, it is kind of a shock how differently your saddle horse will perform compared to working cattle. He will turn quicker and run harder. When we took the left turn out the gate, Bud fell, slamming down onto his chest and stuffed the saddle horn right into my stomach. It hurt, and I was thinking what an inauspicious start this was. (I didn't know it but Goldie fell with Louie right behind me.) We both stayed in the saddle and our horses scrambled up and charged the creek, then up the other side where we could see the herd pulling away. One of the vague instructions of the ranch lady was to press the rear but not too hard, so Lou and I spurred to catch up.

Louie had his chink chaps and a not-too-clean coat on, with his wild rag (as the local cowboys call his silk scarf that is about two feet longer than necessary), and I was wearing my fringed shotgun chaps and my very best clean light gray coat (with a more subdued gray silk scarf, a gift from a young, very beautiful English riding instructor I had attempted to marry Louie off to a few years previous). I tell you this because as we galloped out of the creek bottom to catch the herd, I was amazed to see that my coat was still clean. Then we dove over a small rise and there was a flood pond from the melting snow that was 30 feet across. The last of the herd was just charging out the other side and I thought, "Oh for Christ's sake, here goes my coat," but we slammed through so fast we were out the other side before the muddy drops came back down. I think Lou rode right through my wake.

At this point, our lady leader was about half mile ahead, waiting and watching, so Lou and I put on a ride to show her a Morgan can run, and we can ride, running easily through that broken, snowy, muddy ground, sitting relaxed in the saddle, wondering if we would survive. She held the bunch up in a four-acre catch pen, and then called Lou up front. They led off with Lou riding the downhill side to keep the mares from spilling down, and soon we hit the road up North Brokenback. It was gooey.

When the ground flattened to the sides, Lou dropped back, and we ran hard for about a mile up the slope, with Goldie about to hit the wall. I could hear him laboring and dropping back, but the whole bunch was slowing to a lope and then a trot, so the honor of the Morgan breed was salvaged. About the time we got collected together, the ranch lady bumped the lead right off the side of a red canyon, told Lou to follow them down, and yelled for me to come up.

As Lou disappeared over the side, our cowgirl took off up the road on her leggy quarter horse with me in hot pursuit, and then she started talking to me. My hearing is actually pretty good, considering all the big chainsaws and little airplanes I have interacted with, but I had no clue what she was saying over her shoulder from her hard running horse, so I spurred up a little and then the mud clods from her horse's hooves began flying by on both sides. I knew we were not too far from the end of the trail, so to speak, so I was damned if I was going to ruin my coat just to find out what she had on her mind. I ran between the flying mud balls and watched closely. Soon she pointed at a well-worn trail that dropped off the road toward the bottom of a rim-rock canyon, so Bud and I dove off, pretending we knew what we were doing. We jogged down that steep trail, and soon I saw her off to my left and knew we were blocking in case those mares tried to come back up. Soon we all ended up in the bottom of a very pretty canyon bottom. It was one of those Zane Grey places, down under the high red rim-rock with a little cottonwood-bordered creek running through it. Our horses were steaming. Goldie had an inch of sweat foam on his chest above the breast collar.

The lady followed the bunch up the creek into their winter pasture while Lou and I stepped down by the gate, with Bud and Goldie smoking in the cold mountain air. Lou walked off to pop his freshly greased Aussie whip, and I took my coat off and carefully checked it for mud. It was almost a miracle because there was none.

On the way back down the mountain, our new boss got around to telling Lou and me that she could not pay us for our work as the price of horses was really off. Lou, being a negotiator, tried to trade our work for a couple of pheasant hunts (the place was overrun with them), but she was noncommittal. I was still muttering into my subdued gray silk scarf when we loaded up and left.

END OF PACKING

September 2013

This last two weeks I made what turned out to be the last of my horse-packing trips. I took four archery hunters into Grace Lake from Battle Park and came the closest I have ever come to being killed or totally maimed by three horses.

These horses had only been used once the last two years, and on this trip I over-packed them to accommodate the guys. About a mile out of the trailhead the back horse blew up, slammed the long tent poles he had strapped on his sides into the mare he was tied to and that I was leading on my right side, and she went berserk and passed me and my saddle horse on the left. With the lead going round my hand, it jerked my head down onto that big roping horn while the back horse went by on the right until he hit the end of the tied-off lead from the mare's pack saddle. His breakaway didn't snap, and his lead was just above the hocks on my saddle horse and damned near jerked my horse down.

If Bud, my saddle horse, would have gone down, the

three of them would have stomped me into a bloody mess. As it was, they all tangled up, then stopped with the mare and the back horses heads in my lap and all the leads tight as guitar strings while Bud tap-danced trying to stay on his feet, and me sweet talking them to all stand still 'til we could untangle them

After getting them all collected together, we went about another 100 yards and they went to hell again, but that time they both went crazy on my right side so I was able to jerk Bud into a tight turn to the left, and they fanned out in a big circle until both their packs came apart. I remember seeing two big vodka bottles go skidding across the meadow.

Then, a week later, the hunters called me on a satellite phone and asked me to come get them out of there on Friday. They could call me but I could not call them. I said I'd be in their camp at noon on Friday, so guess what?

When I went out in the dark at 6:30 on Friday morning to catch the horses, we were enjoying our first winter storm. From Deer Haven to Battle Park I ground for over two hours (a fifteen-mile trip) in four-wheel drive. The trees beside the road were weighted down with snow and slamming into the top of the horse trailer and totally freaking the horses out. When I opened the trailer door at Battle Park, the back horse was standing there shaking with his pack saddle under his belly, and so anxious to get out of the trailer he fell on his ass on the icy floorboards.

Staying on the trail the first two miles was pure luck, as it was a white out, and then we came around a corner and bumped into a rider coming out leading one horse. My horses all went crazy, evidently convinced they had never seen anything that scary before. About the time I got them all settled down, the guy's dog came crashing out of the underbrush, and we had some more severe drama. But, his back trail was total luck for me as I would never have found the drop-off down the switchbacks to Grace Lake without that trail to follow, because I was basically riding inside a snowy cloud.

The hunters had evidently convinced themselves I would not make it in, so when I finally stumbled onto their camp in that snowy wilderness, they had not dropped their snow-laden tent or really packed up.

You have not lived till you have torn down and packed up a camp in a foot of fresh snow and 23 degrees, at about 10,000 feet. I was saturated from riding under the snow-laden trees and my fingers were so numb, as were the hunter's when we were packing up, that we had a tiny burner going to temporarily thaw them so we could tie the lash cinches. We flopped the tent, roughly folded with a nice layer of snow still attached, on top the sawbucks.

The trip back out was like a bad dream. I talked one hunter into leading the screwy back horse for a ways to save us another wreck, but that horse's pack just went upside-down anyway not more than 500 yards from their campsite due to the snow-laden tent causing a high center of gravity and frozen lash cinches. And, no burner that time to thaw the fingers.

Then, in the timber the wind started blowing and the trees started shedding their snow loads, and when it came down it was like little microbursts and blizzards combined. My fat, crazy horses thought the world was coming to an end, and I was beginning to believe them. We finally got the packs balanced; I tied the horses together and just rode off and left the hunters.

The trip out of Grace is not really all that far, but this time it seemed to go on forever. The temperature kept dropping, and because I was saturated from the tree-shedding snow, I started getting really cold, and worse even than that, I had to take a leak but there was absolutely no way I was going to stop this train before I got to the trailhead, because that seemed to me an invitation to total disaster, out in snowy Long's Meadow with no trees to tie to. Then, when I finally got to the horse trailer, the lead ropes were so stiff and frozen; tying them up so I could relieve myself was about a half-hour job...or so it seemed. Actually, I didn't so much tie them but rather stuck the yard stick straight frozen leads through the trailer slots with the horses giving me dumb looks.

So there I was, with fingers numb, feeling like oversized sausages and frozen halfway to my elbows and absolutely useless, my coat, chaps and Levis saturated and frozen solid, and needing to pee really badly.

I hate internal conversations, but man I was having one there. I had stripped off my slushy gloves and managed to unsnap my frozen coat far enough to stick my big, fat, frozen fingers into my armpits. I had my legs, encased in frozen long johns, levis and steel-hard frozen shotgun chaps slightly crossed to keep a grip on the old bladder, and was staring between the black tree trunks out into the dirty, gray, snowy sky above the valley to the west.

"Jesus, Cole," my smarter inner self was saying, "You're 71 years old. What in hell are you doing up here?"

That's when my dumber, normal, everyday self said, "Close enough on this packing business."

THE END

Made in the USA
Las Vegas, NV
04 April 2022

46864732R00066